THE JOY OF DIVORCE

FROM CONDEMNATION TO GRACE

A PERSONAL WALK SEEING THE GRACE

OF GOD THROUGH MY DIVORCE

by Peter Sinish and Michael Smith

THE JOY OF DIVORCE

FROM CONDEMNATION TO GRACE

ISBN   978-0-578-50957-0

scripture references are taken from New International Version Bible

(New Spirit Filled Life Bible)

copyright 2002 ,2014

Cover Design

Kayla Schwartz

Formatter

Reggie Kee

Ink Well Spoken

printed in the United States of America

"In our culture the word divorce is never mentioned alongside joy! In fact, in the church culture, the word divorce is almost like winning the lottery. That is the lottery that blackballs you from ever being considered anything but a second-class citizen whose life is now just surviving to the end because of a failed marriage. The Joy of Divorce is a much needed, work on helping people see that divorce, although painful and not wanted, is not the end, but can be a great new beginning. What is refreshing to me as I read this book is the author's ability to take us through the journey of all the emotions, thoughts and obstacles that one goes through with the stigma of divorce in our society. Every person that lives, has a history of that life, and every history brings with it certain baggage that the person carries with them. In *The Joy of Divorce*, the reader will certainly identify with the baggage that comes with a failed marriage, but will also hopefully learn how to deal with and discard unwanted baggage. The Joy of Divorce is about a journey, a journey through hurt and pain, and a journey to find freedom on the other end. Even though this book is dealing specifically with divorce, the material within its pages will help anybody see the inner workings of what is going on in their own life. And through taking this journey with the author will be able to come out on the other side in freedom and joy! A magnificent work to help people see that God has the final word in all our troubles, and God's final word is always from His perspective, which is love, joy and peace!

David Hawkins,

Co- pastor of Grace Life Fellowship and Ministries

TABLE OF CONTENTS

INTRODUCTION : GETTING IT

When my friend, Peter Sinish, first asked me to help him re-write his book, I thought, "Okay, Lord -- what's THIS all about?"

You see, I've been a writer ever since I was in high school. It started with poetry (not uncommon for any adolescent boy), but I also became enamored with the school newspaper, quickly earning a by-line and editorship. I've written some essays and short stories over the years. I've journaled. More recently, I've penned autobiographical snippets for fun and submitted letters to the editor to voice my opinion. For quite a while I had a column in a monthly church newsletter called 'While On The Way'.

But a book? That was a format I had not ventured into. Oh, the idea had *always* enticed me. I can't tell you how many times I thought about subjects and titles. About fiction or nonfiction. About pseudonyms versus my given name, Michael Smith, which had always seemed so common and boring.

Yet I'd never sat at my own notebook, typewriter, or computer, and written it. I've had tons of excuses. I had a family to support. I had to work. The kids came first, with all their assorted activities and commitments. I was tired. I would rather play (at the park, a softball game, watch a movie, hike a trail, eat at a restaurant, have a game of cards, break out a board game, veg in front of the TV, *ad nauseum*).

And I can't disavow for a moment the self-condemnation I used to put myself under. I was horribly perfectionist. And that perfectionism used to paralyze me. I just knew that I could never write a book worthy enough for publishing. And of course just being published would never have sufficed. If I wrote a book it would have to be smashingly successful, or what was the use? So I justified my inaction.

But here was a friend, a very good friend, asking for my help. You see, Peter had heard me read some of my works aloud during some social gatherings. And he loved them. He heaped praise on me and my writing ability. He would just stare at me and go, "Wow...". It felt good.

"I'm writing a book on divorce," he said. "The title is *The Joy of Divorce!*" And then his face would wind into that infectious grin as he let out a hearty laugh. "I'm going to need some help, though. Sometimes I can't make much sense out of what I've written! But I just love the way you write and it has such nice flow." Flow is important to Peter.

And so, without having read a word of his writing, I agreed. I was to become a *co-author*.

Once I began reading what Peter had composed up to that point, I knew what he meant. You see, I would characterize Peter as a stream-of-consciousness writer. The words flow into his brain and then onto the paper. It's wonderfully random and abstract. It's like the bold brush strokes of Vincent Van Gogh, or the sublime spillings of Jackson Pollock. In Peter's writing one never knows where the next thought will lead as the thread winds in, out, and around like a marvelous scribble picture. Yet it is whole. It is complete. It fills the mind like the bouquet of flowers fills a room.

Right away, I could see that we would make a good duo. Because I *get* Peter. And you've got to get him to understand him. And in understanding him, I could flesh out and rearrange the scribble picture into a work more accessible to all. To top it off, I had his permission to inject some of 'Michael' into his work. That's when it was my turn to say "Wow…".

Because, you see, I have my own experience in the matter of divorce. I, too, have walked that excruciatingly lonely and forlorn road. I, too, have experienced the grief, the anger, the anxiety, the pain, the failure, and the negativity that surrounds one like a moat. It is also true that I have guiltily felt relief, even gladness, as the ties that bound dissolved. I know from brutal experience the mixed bag that divorce can be.

Mix in religion and the mixed bag can become downright putrid. I mean, I WAS LETTING DOWN GOD!!! What hope could there possibly be for me? I had become a heathen! I had broken my vows. I had been weak. I had been UNFAITHFUL. I had let down my kids, my family, my friends, and my church. When I looked at myself I was dismayed. And I felt foul.

But God….

But God saw me and my divorce in a different light. And through the spectacular vessel that is my friend Peter, I have been encouraged to share that light with the world. Welcome to the *joy* of divorce.

CHAPTER ONE:
THIS LIFE I HAVE, DIVORCE AND ALL

The Joy of Divorce. I hope I got your attention with that title. I imagine that in your mind you may be saying, "Whaaat?! The JOY of divorce? Come on!" But attention piqued, I'm now going to assume that you have either gone through, or are going through, or know someone that has gone through, this life altering trauma.

And let there be no mistake. It is traumatic. The whole process of divorce can leave one miserable and bearing emotional scars that scream for years and years. One's entire life comes into question, with questions that are seemingly unanswerable. *Was I really in love? Did my spouse ever love me? Am I even loveable? How can I ever trust myself again? How will I move forward from this? Am I better off alone? Why do I feel so lonely? AM I WORTH ANYTHING? TO ANYONE? Does GOD still love me?* It's likely that our self-esteem is shot...and equally likely that doubt rules our thoughts. At least it was that way in my case. I've been there and done that.

Yes, there are self-help books. There are well-intentioned friends trying their best to care for us. There are even people we don't know offering comfort and advice. Then, too, there are those weekend retreats for divorcees trying to mend their broken hearts. Shoot! Let's not omit the religious leaders and church family that so lovingly point out our shortcomings, and the pitfalls we may have succumbed to. Maybe we've even been shunned for our own good, giving us time to think and pray about it. Sometimes, some of it felt helpful. Oftentimes, it did not.

The point I am trying to make is that there is actually very little help available to us for this incredibly life-messing drama we've been through. So each of us chooses a healing journey we believe is going to aid us the most. We start trying to do all the right things, make all the right decisions, think all the right thoughts. Yet all the while, we still feel all wrong. All the while we still have a hurt running so deeply down inside us, we wonder if we'll ever be healed enough to trust beginning a new relationship again.

Shortly after my own divorce took place a profound question entered my head, and I believe it was divinely put there. "Do you want to remain smack-dab in the middle of your divorce, surrounded by its pain? Or will you accept My challenge to see it using My perspective, and live through it?" *God had spoken to me in a very loving way, encouraging me to follow Him.*

The decision I made that day has rocked my world. I decided to adopt a realm of thinking and living from God's perspective. I began a journey moving me from a humanistic lifestyle to a mystical and supernatural lifestyle.

This is not a "How To" book, or even a straight set method on how to get through life. This is the story of my personal walk with God, of who I was, of who I've become, and of how a shattering event like divorce can lead to joy when lived in the person of Jesus Christ. Walk with me. Explore this lifestyle. And see why this life I have, divorce and all, is a life I would have no other way.

CHAPTER TWO: MEDOM

We live in a Medom world. "Medom" (pronounced **mee**-dumb) is an expression I've coined over the years. When I use it in conversation it usually evokes a weird look from the person I'm talking with, as if to say, "What are you talking about?!!!" Let me explain.

When I say that we live in a Medom world, I'm saying that we live in a world where everything is centered around "Me". The opposite of Medom is Kingdom, as in the Kingdom of God, where everything is centered around the King, or Jesus. Medom versus Kingdom; self-centeredness versus God-centeredness.

Looking at the majority of divorces it jumps out at me that usually one party or both are totally occupied with Medom thinking. It bore true for me. Here I was, an outstanding Christian, living the best I knew how to, living for God! Accordingly, when some wave came by to rock my boat (as in some unwanted or unexpected life event) my natural reaction was to try and "smooth the sea". My inclination was always to correct my thoughts and ways by making the proper adjustments according to the way I interpreted scripture. That's Medom thinking.

Let's be honest. When my marriage started being a problem, I naturally reverted to the playground rules I knew as a kid. I wanted the problem solved, but I wanted a solution that suited me. It was all about me! I wanted things fixed my way. That's the mindset I was in when d-i-v-o-r-c-e hit my life. And frankly, I believe that my wife was thinking the same way. She wanted a solution that suited her. Without going into specifics, she had encountered some major situations that needed her attention. And after going through them, she could only see one way out. Her way. Of course her way was not my way. Her thoughts were not my thoughts. We were each stuck in the Medom mindset; unable to accept each other's values, unable to see the other's point of view, stuck without compassion for each other's hurts, and not willing to bend.

So there we were. It seemed our options had been reduced to just one solution. We may not have wanted to, but we accepted each other's Medoms. The judge asked if there was any possibility of reconciliation. We both said "No." We became divorced.

I began the walk of accepting this new thing, this divorce. I tried hard to look at the situation through the eyes and thoughts of Jesus. Try as I might, it was still quite tempting to blame her for everything that had happened to us. Then it became tempting to blame myself! But God kept calling me back to the nature of His heart; to His disposition toward His created people *regardless of what they have done or what their behavior*; to His grace. This was tough for me! It seemed that all circumstances were against me. In my Medom brain I saw everything I had worked for dissolve in front of my eyes. Gone were my business, my home, my security, *my wife*.

I believe that I still had a deep desire and longing to be accepted by God. And it's that desire that drove me to work harder and harder to please God. Yet all the trying never fulfilled that desire.

Still, that's where I was at. My thinking was that God could take my situation into His hands so that I would be healed.

So I set about doing my part. I prayed more. I studied more. I prayed MORE and I studied MORE! But it didn't work. Slowly it dawned on me...it wasn't working because it wasn't what He wanted me to do. *What He wanted from me was to rest, and see the situation through His eyes.* When I finally became still, I could hear Him telling me to look at it from His perspective, not mine. As I continued to listen, I heard it over and over again. It began to play over and over again in my head...His perspective, not mine. Finally one day it sank into my heart and I stopped. I stopped viewing the situation from Medom. I stopped saying to myself that to look at it from a Kingdom perspective was illogical. I moved from Medom to Kingdom, and as I did I realized that looking through God's eyes was a truth in my heart. Moreover, I realized that *He had already made it possible for me to see as He sees.*

From that point on, I knew God had given me the ability to forgive her, and myself, for the ways we had treated each other. There was no more blaming in my heart...only forgiving. Forgiving in just the same way that Jesus forgives each one of us for our myriad screw-ups.

Can I go back to Medom? Can I go back to that place of bitterness and hurt? Yes, I can. Do I go back? The honest answer is that sometimes I do. But that's when the King steps in, and I realize my heavenly Father is there to protect me and love me through any feeling I have. As I write this book I hope to impart the love of the Father and what He has given to each of us in abundance.

CHAPTER THREE:

GRAVEYARDS FROM THE PAST

Let's talk about forgiveness.

It can take a very long time to forgive someone you blame for ruining your life. What comes to mind is ALL THOSE YEARS. All those years of dreaming and building. All those years of saving and sacrificing. All that time spent envisioning and believing in a future of bliss and harmony together. And then...WHAM! It's over. All those years...wasted. Yes, it can take a long, long time to look at THAT PERSON and say "I forgive you."

But let's assume you get to that point...the point in time when you can finally forgive your former partner. That means that you've gotten to the point where *you're the only one left*. And you look at yourself and say, "Can I forgive myself?"

Being in my sixties now I personally know many forced-by-divorce single people. They are just like me. So many of them are stuck on how badly they were treated or how it was all their spouse's fault. Some may even be shamefully admitting, "Yes...I may have had a role in our problems." On any given day, depending on mood or company kept, any of these backtracks are interchangeable. Stated bluntly, **these people have not forgiven**. Oh, they may think they have. They may say they have. And maybe they've even tried. *Tried hard*. But they haven't really once-and-for-all forgiven. And the proof is in their own lives. They are continually living a life that has them utterly bound. If you cannot openly and freely say, "I forgive me, and I forgive you," then you are bound. And the binding is to your past. Your future is on "hold". You can't get to it because you're still bound to the perceived reasons for the divorce. You're stuck to your past.

What does that get any of us? It leads directly to lack of trust in ourselves and in others. Conversely, it also leads to mistrust by anyone wanting to build a new relationship with us. It's a double whammy.

I believe this is where the Medom arose in my life. It happened like this. Being unable to forgive, I was also unable to trust. That mistrust became all encompassing. Unable to maintain a wedded relationship which I presumed was based on Kingdom principles, I felt forced to reconsider my perspective. I decided that trusting was not a good idea. I balked at the Kingdom perspective. That left me with just one option. Medom. I turned to myself. I turned to self-satisfaction. I turned to self-preservation. I became centered around me.

Let's look closer at my life for a moment. My profession taught me how to be adept at fitting into any situation. I became an expert at expressing only what fit into each individual setting. That was the nature of my business. But deep down I knew I was being a chameleon. Deep down I knew that what people saw on the outside did not match my inside. This fact became more exaggerated after my divorce. I was hurting, but also hiding it really well. On the outside I was very caring and giving towards others. But inside, I was at best uninspired, knowing that I was only playing a role and not being myself. My mistrust became a prison. One that left me daring not to acknowledge the sour feelings I carried regarding others and myself. Outside, I had to be alive. But inside I felt dead.

Eventually, I realized that I could not be myself and be unforgiving at the same time. I had become exhausted with my charade. I wanted to be myself. I wanted to live out of my true identity. And I realized that my true self was both a wonderful creation and good. Ultimately, my Medom outlook had failed. I needed to get back to the Kingdom. So I began the trek of truly forgiving myself and my ex.

This turn in my thinking came about because of the question God had so perfunctorily asked me: *Would I start looking at things from His perspective*? Throughout my early years I'd held the opinion that God loved me and wanted nothing but the best for me. But I also grew up in the 60's. I grew up loving trees and bees and drugs and rock'n'roll. Not to mention the spiritual experimentation going on all around me. I became involved with cults and the occult, and I was undoubtedly an agnostic or an atheist (not sure which). I got away from the "God loves me" thing. Yet I still thought I knew who God was, when I actually didn't know Him at all.

Then I had an experience that can only be described as "supernatural". I was saved. That is, the truth of Jesus Christ was revealed to me by God and I became a believer. In one fell swoop my addictions and physical handicaps were taken from me in a 45 minute deliverance that ended with a Jesus worship service. Following that experience, I spent the next 9 months largely by myself. In that time I learned how to pray and live in the salvation of Christ. I began a journey that saw me seeking more and more of God, but only by way of Jesus. My attitude changed. I got back to *knowing* God loved me. *Knowing* that God had me on His mind. *Knowing* that God was my protector and my guide.

But did I let Him guide me, protect me, even love me? The truth is, being early in my revelation, I only let Him help me some of the time. I mean, I knew God was great at the saving stuff, but as far as the rest of my life, I thought He could use my help. Plus I somehow got the notion that if I did the right stuff He would be pleased with me and give me what I asked for. Sound familiar? So when I received this call from Him to try His perspective, I turned it into "Oh boy! Something really cool is going to happen now! I'm going to get some of that good stuff called Grace!"

Having been somewhat versed in Jesus growing up meant that I had also heard of Grace. As defined for me, Grace meant *highly favored by God*. "So," I said to myself, "if I am living in God's Grace, that must mean that I am highly favored by God! And everything I desire is going to come to pass!" How Medom is that! I was never taught that Grace was about relationship, both with God and with others. I only knew that I was highly favored and...end of conversation. At this point I could become quite self-righteous. If other people didn't understand how highly favored I was, I would beat them over the head with it. I would use bible verses as interpreted by me to prove my point. Frankly, I was more than willing to accept Grace, but sorely lacking in the giving of Grace.

Slowly, I began looking at people through His eyes. God *loves* His creation. It's all there in the Genesis story--that upon completing His work, He rested with His creation. He walked with Adam and Eve. He talked to them. He walked with mankind, and loved on mankind, because it was His desire to do so. Okay, okay, we all know the story. But even after what might be termed a 'major screw-up' on our part, He still called out to His creation. He still wanted to have a relationship with them. The Bible is a love story about the sweet relationship He wants with you and me. He even had a plan to accommodate the 'screw-up' by sending His son as a sacrifice so that we may again live in deep fellowship with Him. A fellowship so deep that He actually lives *in* us. Jesus in us. Jesus, the highly favored Son of God. Jesus, the Grace in us. Grace through Jesus. Grace becomes the cornerstone, embodying the love that God has for each of us; Grace to live a life of abundance; Grace as healing, as peace, as joy, as completeness. I began to see this whole thing had nothing to do with me but everything to do with the love that God had for me. I began to see that He loved me even in the midst of a sloppy, destructive divorce. *His Grace even covered that!*

The church I grew up in taught that I had to walk a pretty straight and narrow line to receive this Grace. But when I began observing mine and everyone else's life from God's point of view, I started to understand that it was because of His great love for each one of us that we were given Grace. When He gave us Jesus, He gave us high favor. And I began to understand that we really do not have to work for it. The only thing we have to do is receive it for the gift it is. All we need do is accept what has already been given to us.

I began to see the love that God our Father has for my ex-wife. While it is true that He does not like divorce, it is also true that He loves the people involved regardless. His love is unconditional. Regardless of our behavior He always loves us. He loves us... He loves us... He loves us. As we become aware of this reality we begin forgetting about ourselves and our Medoms. We start seeing people from God's eyes and heart.

So many people, with no respect to background, have been taught a different way to survive in this world. Lists of rules and regulations, of do's and don'ts, have been embedded into them. People have been taught that if they do this or do that in just the right manner, then rewards await. But the reward is at the top of whichever ladder they've chosen to climb. 'They' (whoever 'they' are) tell us that as long as we follow each rule and measure each step, we'll succeed and live a merry ole life. 'They' say, "It's a dog eat dog life," and that if you want to have any chance in this life you'd better live it the way 'they' say to live it. I'm not trying to chide who 'they' are. I respect that their rules to live a successful life are held very strongly. Much of that teaching has been handed down, generation to generation, for centuries upon centuries.

I can even see where this design to attain the good life originated. It was when the angel Lucifer (who later became known as Satan) wanted to be like God. Lucifer decided he wanted to be independent from his creator and work his way into power. That power can be so alluring. One reason I latched onto the occult earlier in my life was because I believed it gave me power over people. With such power I could tell them what to do, where to go, etc. And if they didn't succumb to my power, I made them pay dearly. Of course, I did not recognize that I was Satan's puppet.

During a divorce our minds seem tossed to and fro by thoughts that disagree with each other. "I should have done this," or "I should have done that," and if only I had then this divorce never would have happened. Such thoughts are not focused on the Spirit of God. They are focused on me. Those thoughts have been groomed by society. Our actions, dictated by tortured emotions, move us to chaos. When the drama diminishes, we reflect on our regrettable past. During lulls in the torment we hide in the illusion that we've escaped--that we're somehow safe and secure in our Medom realm. But it is all Houdini trickery, as we are all too soon re-inundated by torrents of condemnation, drowning in doubt. Trust is as elusive as the wind. Once again, trying to be 'our own person' results in failure, and we trust no one.

The temptation to return to Medom can be strong. In the Old Testament it is well documented that man wanted rules to live by and a king to rule over them (1 Sam 10:17-19). It was their free will at work. Since God gave us free will, He said, "Okay, here you go!" And off we were. The only trouble was that man couldn't keep the rules, and neither could the King! In spite of this, God knew the hearts of His creation. He knew their desires and that ultimately they desired Him. He knew they desired union with Him. But He also knew His people would never achieve union with Him via the law. Yet His love for His creation endures forever. And even though they could not keep His commandments, His heart was still all for them.

When Jesus came, He brought with Him the means to fulfill the hearts of God's people. With His sacrifice on the cross, He fulfilled the law that no man could. And as He walked the earth, Jesus refuted the stance that any method or works or 'climbing the success ladder' could reconcile people to God. As He hung on the cross at Calvary he cried out, "IT IS FINISHED!" (John 19:30). He paid the price that no man could pay for the cleansing of our sin. The curtain in the temple was torn from top to bottom, giving each of us the access to God that Adam and Eve had before the fall. Jesus died so that we may have new hearts; so that we may have the Spirit of God within us; so that we may dwell in the Kingdom while living on the earth (Ezek 36:26-27).

We must realize how God sees us; how He has always looked upon us. Let us remember that He loves us. He created us. He desires fellowship with us. In the Lord's Prayer it states, "My Kingdom come on earth as it is in heaven." It seems to me from that quote that God is beckoning to us NOW. He desires communion with us *on earth even as we will have it in heaven.*

As we become affirmed in God's perspective about us, we toss the old Medom thoughts out of our minds. We are transformed. God's thoughts become our thoughts. We glean that we are good, not evil; that we have peace, not disarray; that we are righteous and holy, not deceitful and unclean. These are only a sampling of how our minds become transformed. The God perspective is a far cry from what most people in society grow up with. But as we gain it, we remember to say "NO" to Medom. We remember the Kingdom; that the Bible is a love story inspired by the Holy Spirit describing how God is loving us back to Him; that He cares about us; that He's not lying in wait to hammer the heck out of us when we screw up. It's why He sent Jesus, to pay for all our sins, past, present, and future. When God sees us He sees Jesus His beloved in us. Our Spirit is ever-alive and our Spirit-man is made perfect in Christ. Without Jesus, our mind focuses on ourselves. Enter Jesus' love. God's mind rests on love.

As I stopped dwelling in the Medom of my mind, I started to see my ex-wife as God sees her. Looking past her imperfections, I see a daughter of God who is perfectly made. I see a woman seeking the true identity of God and her true nature in Him. I see her coming to *know* how He thinks of her. When I arrived at this stage of my own spiritual journey, I *knew* I could and would forgive her. Knowing I am forgiven gives me strength to forgive, just as knowing I am loved gives me strength to love. I am not the Judge, for if I am, I will be judged. No thanks. Still, I suffered from the delusion that I was a judge until I acquired His eyesight.

Do I think this way every day, every moment? No. But my mind is being transformed. My thoughts are becoming like God's. I have great freedom because of this. Firstly, I am not holding my ex accountable -- which means I truly desire the best for her. Secondly, being no longer bound by the chains of unforgiveness, I am able to enjoy a life of adventure, peace, and hope. As the apostle Paul states, I forget the past and move to the mark set for me. I cannot press on to God's true calling by going back to graveyards of the past.

CHAPTER FOUR: BECOMING NOAH

I became Noah.

Oh, not literally, of course. But figuratively speaking, I entered a stage of my divorce that mirrored Noah's life. Noah's story became for me an example of how Grace lifts one above the law and into a place of rest.

So take yourself back, if you will, to Noah's time. It's an early time in mankind's history, when the earth was still largely unspoiled. The vastness of God's creation, green and lush, still dominated the dry land. In the vast fields and forests huge numbers of wild beasts and tiny fauna roamed unhindered and mostly uninterested in men and their deeds. Needs were simple. Life was day to day. A man, or an animal for that matter, needed water and food, and a shelter for rest and protection. It was a daily struggle. Men's homes were made of earth, stone, and wood. There were no electronic technologies, no machines, and no knowledge of anything save what one could physically see.

But just like today -- there were distractions. Both then and now, God's own creation, Man, becomes easily distracted. For "the human population began to grow rapidly on the earth. The sons of God saw the beautiful women of the human race and took any they wanted as their wives." (Gen 6:1 NLT). There were distractions! Men reveled in their flesh. Men became utterly distracted from who they were as Spirit beings. They became obscenely gross. "Then the Lord saw that the wickedness of man *was* great in the earth, and *that* every intent of the thoughts of his heart *was* only evil continually." (Gen 6:5 NKJV). God saw the corruption of the people. Just how do you think God felt about that? Let's continue with scripture.

"And the LORD was sorry that He had made man on the earth, and He was grieved in His heart." (Gen 6:6 NKJV). God felt sad. Even more, He felt distressed about this Man He'd made. For all their thoughts had become consistently and totally perverted. Men had completely distracted themselves with the consummation of their carnal desires. And despite the fact that God knew the WHOLE story -- past, present, and future -- He still grieved, and decided it was time for a change. A drastic change. Like a nearly "extinction level event" change.

"But Noah found favor with the LORD." (Gen 6:8 NLT). Noah was given Grace. And a whole bunch of instructions on how to build an ark. BUILD A WHAT? WHAT'S THAT?!!! I can see Noah scratching his head in bewilderment. Yet by faith he heard the voice of God and obeyed Him in pursuance of this adventure. In other words, Noah began construction because of his trust in God, and his continued spiritual communion with God. Noah started building.

Let me pause here to describe how I started to become Noah. You will probably agree with me that divorce hurts. From an assured and placid sea of matrimony rose great swells of turmoil. Emotions that previously had no life welled within me. I was suddenly confronted by betrayal, doubt, and misgiving. My flesh yearned to let my emotions take rein. So I let my carnal desires flood my being. A deluge of hurt and pain washed over me. I became angry, sad, and disillusioned with God and my community. Who wouldn't? It's how the flesh reacts.

My animalistic instincts kicked in and I went into survival mode. My answer to the pain was to bury my hurting heart. It felt good to bury it and it felt right. It felt like the salve I needed. It also allowed me to feed my carnal need to be independent. In my mind I became an "island unto myself". I sought refuge on an island of denial, where I was unreachable, untouchable, unhurtable. If there was a sign on my island, it would have read, "I'm fine. Leave me alone."

But if I may be so bold, let me say this. God stepped in. And like Noah, **I found favor with the LORD**. Favor came suddenly and majestically. It came lovingly and wonderfully. I didn't know I needed it. I didn't know I wanted it. Yet it came, even though I didn't ask for it.

Though at first my sole concentration had been about my own satisfaction, and even though it may have seemed gratifying to satisfy myself, I knew in my heart it was self-serving. I was working hard at deceiving myself. I wasn't living by the law written on my heart. I was living by the stone tablets. I had been distracted to live by the stony heart of my pre-Jesus days. Hey, it happens. I had been mortally wounded, and I reacted with mortal combativeness. My flesh felt like the only reality I knew and I was going to do everything I could to defend myself.

But I found favor with the LORD. I was given Grace. I was reminded of my spirit-nature, my Jesus-nature, my rebirth in Him. I was given a chance to take a new action. One given to me by God. A chance to receive, and respond differently. So I said, "Yes!" to Grace, and decided to trust Him. I started building.

Now, for Noah, it was building a giant boat. For me, it was building my relationships. Bear with me now. Let's make the ark a symbol, and the name of that symbol is GRACE. Noah, his family, and the animals were all lifted up in protection by the ark (GRACE), and rode above the turmoil of the earth. They were not affected by the rain (which we could label JUDGMENT) but instead rose to live in an atmosphere of Grace within the confines of the ark. I, too, was lifted to life by Grace. I, too, was lifted above the "rain" of my divorce. But just like Noah, I needed to be patient.

To begin with, it must have stunk to high heaven on that ark. But so did my relationship with my ex. Still, imagine the joy they must have felt on that wooden ship, knowing they had been spared. I am sure that Noah and his clan were constantly in worship, constantly in reverent awe of the work God was doing. And so was I. Because of God's unmerited favor, I was given new eyes. I saw my soon-to-be ex in a new light. The stench that had filled my nostrils dissipated and left. I was able to take a deep breath and smile.

But the *adventure* (as opposed to the *ordeal*) was far from over. First there were the 40 days of downpour, when the flood covered all the earth. Then God sent a wind to blow across the water and the water began to evaporate. But it wasn't until 12½ months later that Noah saw that the land was dry and gave the order to leave the boat.

So, too, my divorce took time. After the initial blow, there was aftermath. It took months to complete the process. It takes time to grieve and to heal. But all during that time, I rested in God's Grace. I rested in God's good work for me in the ark.

Because of the favor bestowed on him, Noah was allowed to live apart from the devastating drama occurring on the earth. "Noah was a righteous man, the only blameless man living on the earth at the time. He consistently followed God's will and enjoyed a close relationship with Him." (Gen 6:9) His needs were being met supernaturally, first in the building of the boat, and then abiding within it. Likewise, as we accept the free gift of Grace from the Father, we are placed in protection from the floods that disrupt our lives. We build out of faith, and then the faith resides in us. We become the boat! As we receive the Grace into us, we not only become Noah -- we become the ark as well!

In us is everything we need to live a life of abundance. Our need for peace, our need for joy, our need for security -- all our needs are met as we become a vessel for the One who is Grace. As we walk in and rest in the boat of Grace, we rise above any circumstances. We are not of this world but live in it. Noah chose by faith to build an ark for personal protection. We choose to accept what has been built for us by Jesus, and thus acquire the ultimate protection in this natural life.

Look at one example from Jesus' life here on earth, an example showing that He Himself lived and walked in protection. In Nazareth, Jesus asserted to the people in His hometown synagogue that while He knew there were many that needed healing, it would not be happening.

Why? Because "...the truth is, no prophet is accepted in his own hometown." (Luke 4:24) The narrative goes on to say that the worshipers became furious at Jesus' comment. So furious that they mobbed Him intending to push Him over a cliff! "But He slipped away through the crowd and left them." (Luke 4:30) Jesus was protected. Even He dwelt in and amidst Grace (because He is Grace) while on His human passage.

All because of who God is. He is Love. And He extends Grace to one and all that will receive it. He is the God that bestowed Grace upon Noah. He's the Father that communed with Jesus while He lived upon the earth. He's the same God that puts us in Grace and Grace in us so that we might gratefully enjoy His protection, exuberance, and tranquility.

You see, for me it all comes down to the heart. God's heart for Noah is the same heart He has for me. A heart overflowing with love. Too, in God's redemptive plan, there is a new heart for all of us -- the heart of Christ. We don't have a heart of or for sin. Because of Jesus' sacrifice we live under the constant showering of the Father's love. Because of God's offering of Grace we can live in abundance no matter the circumstances. Just like Noah. And it's all because of who our unchanging God is. He is the God that bestowed Grace on Noah. The God that gives Grace to us through Jesus. The God that removed my heart of death and gave to me instead a heart of everlasting life.

"Noah was a righteous man" and, by Jesus, so am I! So are we! Only because of the Grace of God.

CHAPTER FIVE:
GROWING THE UNDERDOG

Looking back on my life I notice that I have always been for the underdog. Perhaps it was because that's how I saw myself. I grew up the youngest of other brothers in my family, and from an early age I felt a need to gain my brothers' approval. In order to do that I needed to perform and perform well. I think it's a common thing to yearn for acceptance by others. And too, to try and earn it.

In any event I found that as I grew I always wound up rooting for the person that had the odds stacked against them. I found that I would wantonly stand up to people that bullied or oppressed others. I would stand up for them even when they either couldn't or wouldn't. Today I would say I acted out of mercy for them. I also found that I was able to forgive people that had made blunders in their lives. My assumed underdog identity made it easy for me to put myself in their shoes, and have compassion for them when others would not.

Now we all know what defending the weak gets us, right? Ya -- a whole lot of battles and disagreements. To this day I still struggle with this trait of mine. I say struggle because even though I might see my actions as being beneficial to others, they can in fact be detrimental to my personal relationships.

Concerning my divorce, it was a very logical (dare I say, merciful) step for me to forgive the transgressions my wife had made. It was a part of my underdog persona. Also, I had enough spiritual sense to know that forgiving her released me from judging her, which in turn freed me to address my own guilt and condemnation without any influence from her.

Looking back on that scene, I probably seemed very cold. I had constructed an imaginary wall around myself in an effort to feel protected from the feelings associated with the divorce. The wall also prevented me from being warm. I believe I was congenial, but guarded. After all, it wasn't like I'd harbored some secret desire to get divorced. I didn't want a divorce. It was being thrust on me. At that point it seemed completely natural to go into underdog mode. In my mind it made all the sense in the world to build a wall.

But a significant difference occurred in my thinking from the underdog undertakings of my childhood. While growing up I could never understand why people chose to pick on the weak or mistake-prone. It bugged me. People like that bugged me! Now a new perspective began to emerge for me. God's perspective. I started to become aware of *why* my wife had made the decisions she had. I started to understand *why* she was doing what she was doing. And by God, my heart went out to her. *When one focuses on Jesus, one can forgive with compassion.* Plus there was an added bonus -- the compassion sent out warmed *my* heart! Living in Jesus' forgiveness, I can understand why a person responds or reacts the way they do. In His forgiveness I will not judge, but will see beyond the fault and see the hurt.

On a chalkboard in my kitchen is the following statement: "A mistake is just misguided good." I have pondered often how that applies to my divorce. Is that statement an accurate reflection of how God sees divorce? When a couple makes the decision to divorce -- is it a case of misguided good?

In my case, we thought it best to separate for awhile before we talked about a possible reconciliation. During the separation she discovered new facets of herself and embarked on new ventures. All I knew was I missed her and wanted her to come home where she belonged. She offered that she would agree to ending the separation, but with a big *IF*. Her stipulation was that her new lifestyle would be her first priority, and that activities related to that lifestyle would be her second and third priorities. I came in fourth, along with the church. I thought about this for a bit, but it didn't take me long to realize I couldn't accept being fourth. I said no to her offer, explaining, "You are my wife, and we are to live in unity." In other words I was saying, "No way, honey. I'm putting you first, so you need to move me up the ladder to the top rung, too." To this, she said no. Divorce it would be.

Boy was that hard for me to swallow! We had been married 17 years. We were deeply invested in a business together. I had always envisioned us together in the future. But somehow it all fell apart.

Then my soon-to-be-ex made a statement that blindsided me. She said, "I have not lived in faith for a long time. I was living in your faith, Peter." I never realized how broken we'd become. Perhaps I had been wrapped up in a very time consuming business for too long. As I allowed for rumination on her declaration, I started to see her through my Father's eyes. My perspective changed and my heart went out to her with the compassion of Jesus. I saw that she had lost her faith focus. She was no longer confident in her own walk with Jesus. Her situation reminded me of the bible verse, "Be careful! Watch out for attacks from the Devil, your great enemy. He prowls around like a roaring lion, looking for some victim to devour." (1 Pet 5:8 NLT). I believe it is a fact that keeping one's eye on the deceiver assures that one will be deceived. She had taken her eyes off of Jesus. Somehow, the circumstances of our life and the things of this world had pried her focus away from Him.

Enter our religious life. We had spent our entire marriage in service to the local church. That meant regular attendance and lots of work. It meant following commandments. There was to be no drinking, no swearing, and a whole bunch of other "no's". It meant doing everything by The Book. When we messed up our religious commitment, we would ask for forgiveness and get back on the 'Godly Life' treadmill. And a treadmill it was. Here is a sampling of our church life. We were both on the Praise & Worship Team which meant lots of practice. She babysat the pastor's children. I was a member of multiple men's groups and also belonged to an intercessory prayer team. We attended major faith conferences. We became very involved in a 'deliverance' ministry. We studied the Word so that we could know it, quote it, understand it, and believe it (we thought). All that, and the witnessing of Godly miracles occurring amongst us as well. *Divorce was not supposed to happen to a Christian couple like us! Where did we go wrong?*

Yet there I was in my Medom initiating a divorce proceeding. Ultimately I saw the whole thing as a big project to complete. I challenged myself to get through it with as little emotion as possible.

Spiritually, my attitude was "Keep it in the present." Having forgiven her, and having been shown the root of our troubles, I was released to look at myself. There were no hooks in me to drag me around. The past was the past. I was confronted with having to forgive myself for the past I'd created. I had to deal with guilt and condemnation trying to creep in. I knew the bible verse, "There is therefore now no condemnation to those who are in Christ Jesus..." (Rom 8:1 NKJV). But I couldn't help wondering...did that hold true in the case of divorce? I reasoned that God knew the situation. Not that he allowed the situation, but that he knew of human weakness. I thought maybe that knowledge would pacify me. But no, there was no solace in that.

Then it hit me. God, by the blood of Jesus, has forgiven *all* of my sins, past, present, and future; and if what I did was a sin (that is if the divorce was a sin) so what? It doesn't matter! I AM forgiven BY HIM. Who am I to hold a higher standard to myself than God? That road leads straight to Medom! Another verse loomed in my mind. "...so are my ways higher than your ways and my thoughts higher than your thoughts," (Is 55:9 NLT). Why was I holding myself in bondage to MY thoughts when HIS thoughts led to freedom!

I left town. I just had to leave. In the middle of the divorce proceeding, I knew I had to get away from the place we had lived for so long. I was having trouble seeing the forest for the trees and I was being called into the woods. I headed to Vermont for the Fall season to work at a country inn. I was a good 30 miles from the closest church, which was down a mountainside and across a valley.

Thank God! Thank God that church was 30 miles away and out of my reach. Because I really didn't want to go to church! So when a trace thought would whistle through my mind that I *should* go to church, there was enough distance that I would not go.

I was blessed to be staying in a cottage, lent by a friend, that overlooked the mountains of Vermont. God had me right where He wanted me: alone with Him. My spiritual eyes became wide again seeing the beauty of the land. I began to realize that the church life I had been leading was all about pleasing the people around me. The Worship Band was about us helping the congregation draw closer to God. The music was about building a platform from which the pastor could speak to His people. My deliverance ministry was supposed to get people away from physical, emotional, and spiritual attacks. Actually it was placing pressure on them to perform in certain ways by doing certain things, which in turn led them straight back under attack! All the conferences, the meetings, the 'must do' service, all the *works! It all led to bondage.*

I realized I had been called away from my church to see its religiosity for what it was and how it operated. And it broke my heart. I saw that the church had set up a bunch of rules centered around self and not around Christ. Somehow, immersed in all that 'churchiness', my life had changed from focusing on God to focusing on myself. Sure, belief in Jesus was there, and belief in God's realm was there -- but I saw that there were still places in my realm where I hadn't let God in. *Seeing this moved me to a mode of freedom I had not experienced in 30 years of being born again.* I saw the entirety of my life in a new light. I had not been operating out of the pure motivation provided by God's love. I saw that I had molded my family into a machine of 'doing'. Heartbreakingly, that 'doing' led to its dissolution.

My big question was answered. The reason we were divorcing was that we had not allowed the Spirit of God to rule in our lives. We knew the verse, "...Christ in you, the hope of glory," (Col 1:27); we knew it well in our heads, but we had not let it sink down to dwell in our hearts. We had hoped for security in rules, and wound up completely unsecured.

My Vermont respite was over. I had to get back to my hometown and deal with the situations I had put on hold. Truth be told, I did not want to deal with this past life I had been leading, for I knew what its worldly outcome was to be. My house was in foreclosure. My business was in liquidation for a meager amount. My car was being repossessed. And I would soon be an older single man, alone in the world. It would have been easy to be depressed. But instead, I WAS HAPPY with the new heart-felt knowledge that my God was MY GOD, and that He was living in me.

Back in town, I ran into an old friend of mine who had started a small church. He asked me to join him in the venture. I said yes and quickly became loyal to the man. After listening to my story and learning about everything I had gone through, he asked if I'd share my testimony via a series at the church. I agreed and began letting people know about this very recent revelation in my life, and how in spite of my circumstances I could be so happy.

Was I in for a surprise. A few weeks into the series I was asked to stop. And the reason blew me away. I was told that what I was sharing was unbiblical. Really. Unbiblical. In my estimation, I would say that I was sharing my re-evaluation of the Grace of God. I would say that I was sharing a truth about God that had risen from the ashes of my divorce encounter. But what they heard was heresy. The experience showed me that even when the Church knows it needs something, and is shown what it needs, it will reject the message if it necessitates personal change.

So as quickly as I had been asked into this church, I was asked even quicker to leave. No worries. My Father in Spirit immediately gave me new direction. I went to another church with the instruction to "go get completely healed." Now this is just so interesting. It still puts a grin on my face to think about it. Because no sooner had I introduced myself in this new church than the pastor there gave the word to everyone, "Peter needs to be left alone...do not minister to him...do not ask him to do anything...just let him be." I was allowed to rest and renew. And things remained that way for two years. Two years of being re-cultured into the completed work of the cross. Time enough to grasp that each one of us is a unique creation of God and that He loves us no matter what we do. Time to know that there is nothing we can do to make Him love us more. He is love. And He loves us. No more striving for love; no more conditional love; nothing to do except believe in His love and accept it. The more we know God's love for us and understand what He thinks of us, the more we are loosed from pasts that haunt us.

No more am I that person who performs to win approval. Today I accept my Father's love, and thus need not perform for people. I have my Daddy's love and that is all I need. As my mind is transformed by this truth, past hurts metamorphize into Grace living through me; a Grace spilling onto the lives of those around me. No longer am I the underdog. Nor is anyone who receives the gift of God's Grace in Jesus.

The divorce went smoothly through the court process. The judge asked us both if this was what we wanted. Rather hesitantly, we both said yes. She went on to her new priorities and I -- well I went on to live in the wonder and enchantment that is God.

CHAPTER SIX: SEX AND THE DIVORCEE

Ugh. Who hasn't reminisced about the making of love from a marriage in the past? Personally, my ex and I had succeeded in abstaining from sex before we were married. That was quite a challenge to say the least! But we made it until after the ceremony, and then the enjoyment began. And boy do I mean enjoyment! Sex in marriage is a joy. Not only the act itself, but the looking forward to it. Shoot, it was fun. Myself, I'm a sensual guy. I wanted to make love a lot. And we did for many years.

Then all of a sudden it stopped. Her issues, my issues, the very issue of divorce -- they all thrust themselves upon our physical intimacy. The frequency of our sexual encounters took a nosedive into almost complete disappearance. My former enjoyment vanished as the act turned obligatory. Then we were separated. The final papers were signed. And the sex was over. It was a done deal.

I began to live life alone again. Alone in bed. You know, just going to bed by myself was weird! Without trying, the fantasies came. The memories arose, and the struggles began.... How was I to tame this desire welling up within me? This desire that now could not be fulfilled? My mind would race with the idea that I had to kill these thoughts. But how? I was too proud, or maybe too filled with self-condemnation, to ask anyone. The only answer that came to mind was that if my body were to release its seed, then the desire consuming me would end. WRONG. That does not work! That was only a temporary fix that left me wanting as much or more as before. Thus I was constantly being left with the thought that I had to kill the desire.

I was having breakfast with a good friend of mine one morning. During our conversation he mentioned that in the old testament, God worked with the external nature of man. But under the new covenant of Jesus, God deals first with the internal. That's when WHAM, I realized something.

Remember when the Israelites were moving into their new home in Canaan? Do you also remember what was often God's explicit instructions to them? In case you don't -- it was to kill EVERYTHING...men, women, children, animals...everything. Furthermore, they were told several times not to take any of the conquered people's possessions for their own.

First of all, I cannot imagine the bloodbath that resulted from these instructions. On a very human level, such acts would be abhorrent, even uncommittable. So it was only by obedience to God that the instructions could be carried out. Secondly, such instructions searingly invoke the question "Why?". Why did God tell His chosen people to destroy everything they conquered? Many scholars have suggested, and I also believe, that it was necessary to prevent corruption. Our omnipresent God knew that corruption was inevitable if the Israelites coexisted with either the subdued peoples or their properties. God knew that if the Canaanite women were not killed (that is that if they were not rendered unavailable) there would be inter-marriage with Jewish men. God knew that if Canaanite men were to live they would most certainly desire Jewish women for brides. God knew that to leave any remnant of the former culture was to invite contamination on His people. God cannot abide in contamination. He had provided the Jews with an external way to purify themselves. But there was no way for the Canaanites, so they had to be exterminated.

Ultimately, God was protecting His chosen people from harm not unlike we do with our own children. God is Love, and from love He protects us. In the old testament that love had to be manifested externally. Again, in just the same way that I would kill a snake (or a human) that threatened the life of my beloved child, so God acted from an external realm. It was the nature of the relationship He had with His chosen people. *God rested on them, not in them.*

Jump to the new testament. Jesus died and arose in His glory. *God in us the hope of Glory* (Col 1:27). *Jesus resides in us.* No longer is God external. *He is internal.* When Jesus takes up residence within me, he presides over my mind. Significantly, He does not want to share my mind with the thoughts and actions of my past. In Christ, I have a new nature. I am a new person. I am anew in Him. And being anew, not just in Spirit but now also being united with the mind of Christ, it is His desire to kill off our past habits/lifestyles. I no longer have to do the killing, but *God in Christ is now in a position to do the killing.* He's in me. It's an internal purifying; an internal saving from corruption.

Before Jesus, we lacked the power to change our minds. Our carnal desires would define our acts, even if they did not satisfy. But after Jesus, and with Him in us, we have the power we previously lacked. It is only through His grace and power that we experience our minds being changed. I spent *years* trying to fight this battle. I would win, I would lose, I would win, I would *always* end up losing again. And I would ask Daddy, my Father in heaven, "Why can't I conquer this? I know You want me to, but I just can't do it." There it is again...the Medom thought pattern.

I know I'm not the only divorcee to ever fight this sex battle. I believe that most if not all divorcees have waged the same battle in their own heads. I'm not unique. It was easy for me to focus on my body, mind, and animal instincts. It was too easy for me to lose focus on Jesus. In the moment it can be hard to remember that I don't have to depend on myself. I'm not alone with my thoughts and desires. God knows them. And God loves me even with those thoughts. I was starting to say to myself, "I trust you Lord," *but was I really?* I knew that Jesus loved me, but I'd catch myself wondering if I could really trust Him. I was trying to look at this entire situation through His eyes, BUT....

Sometimes revelation is sudden. It's like a light bulb switching on. But other times it's gentle. God spoke to me in a gentle voice and said, "Trust me, Peter. Rest in the love I have for you. You have grasped it intellectually, but now know it in its reality."

This revelation showed me that I was not unlike the Israelites of old. I am sure there were those Israelites that wondered if they could really trust God, and I could identify with them. It can seem like the answer is to resist. It doesn't seem like the answer is to trust. But here it was being revealed to me. So I began to rest in His love. I stopped striving to learn about it. I stopped expending energy doing things. I stopped laboring and entered quietude. And praise God, I began to feel His love through every molecule of my body. I began to *know* that He really does love me.

I let go of the concerns I had about my lustful thoughts and actions, instead just resting in His love. Yes, my mind would still conjure up visions and major desires, but they did not concern me. All I felt was His love. And in feeling His love, there was no condemnation surrounding my thoughts and actions. I saw His love over and above my performance. And I was at rest with that. No more grinding. No more fretting. No more getting on the Ferris Wheel. Just resting in a new found love that I knew personally.

I continued in this way for some time when suddenly I realized that somewhere along the line, I had lost that desire for sex. It had gone! The verse "For I remember your sins no longer" (Heb 8:12) came into my mind, and it made perfect sense that if He has forgotten them then so can I. The verse does not say that I won't have random thoughts, and I do. The big difference is that rather than wage war against those thoughts, as I did for so many years, I now accept them as random and hardly ponder them. Should a lustful thought try to linger, I remember my revelation of how much My Father loves me, and the thought is vanquished. It doesn't have a chance to survive.

I see women through the eyes of Jesus more and more. I have turned from the external to the internal lifestyle. That's not to say that I don't recognize and admire beauty. I most surely do. But in such a different way. A way that includes the entire depth of the person, all the way to the Spirit.

We are a new creation in Christ who knew no sin. That is our new identity which is taking over our lives. It started in our Spirit and grows from the inside out. The new man in us is killing the mind and habits of our former self as we transform into His new creation.

Sex and the divorcee is no longer an UGH subject for me. Thanks to revelation, trust, and rest, I am not governed by the wiles of my flesh anymore. My Lord is sovereign in me and I accept with humble gratitude His gift of conversion. The external is always there, as is the internal. But it is the internal that is eternal, and where the great change takes place, shaping our lives in wonderful and glorious ways.

CHAPTER SEVEN: WHAT DO I DO NOW?

Once my divorce was finalized, a question loomed: "What do I do now?" All my thoughts of grandeur had been wiped out by the signing of a piece of paper. In a sense, I was bereft, and left by myself. But my mind kept wanting to scream at me, "No! This is not what I want!" Because I knew that what I really wanted was to be married. I knew it in the deepest parts of my heart. When I took the time to remember, way back, to the beginning of the marriage, I would remember that it was good. It was good back then! And I enjoyed having a companion. I would enjoy a companion now.

That's when things really got weird in my mind, as I began pondering the meeting, the flirting, and the starting of a new relationship. AAAGH! To be honest, none of that sounded very grand, or even appetizing. I mean, I believed in the institution of marriage. I believed in all its assorted benefits. But to be sure, I wasn't relishing having to go through ALL THAT PROCESS again. Another mate? Sure. Another date? GRRRRR....

Looking back, I don't think there was anything unusual about my thoughts, my longings, or my angst. In fact, I would characterize it as normal in the wake of a divorce. But let's stop here a moment, so that I may catch you up on the particulars of my case.

You see, I had experienced all this once before. Because this wasn't my first marriage. It was my second. And what I was awakening to in the aftermath of this second marriage was peculiar. I noticed that both of my exes were somewhat of the same character. Here is a sampling of just some of the similarities:

- they'd each been married previously

- they both had children living with them, and

- they were in need of things.

What I mean to say regarding the last is that they were each emotionally handicapped. Their neediness had manifested as a result of their divorces, and their own perceived weakness and fault in those marriages. On top of that, their need had become a constrictor, impeding their lives.

Now what about me? Well, you can call me Mr. Compassion. That's "my" character. It's something I've known about myself for as long as I can recall..." this inner need" I have to help people move along in life. I like to assist them, whether it be physically, financially, or emotionally.

In retrospect, I'm not surprised that I was drawn to the women I married. Yes, there was the initial magnetism. But our chemistries were much more than that. Because, you see, we fit. It was almost as if I sought out "women in need" as a qualification for having a relationship with them. All I had to do was find her, and I would start helping. The woman, out seeking a mate for herself, meets this guy named Mr. Compassion and assumes he is seeking relationship. So, in her mind my helping hand appears as a desire for relationship. And I, in my own need, accept her desire and build a relationship that becomes a marriage. So, it was her need, her hopes and desires -- meeting and being married to -- my need, my mortar and bricks, my blood, sweat, and tears.

Let me stress that this development was mutual. I am not blaming either of my exes for somehow using me or for leading me somewhere I did not want to go. I was the one that accepted the relationship. I had needs that I thought she could satisfy. So, my flesh would cry out, "She's the one! She'll complete me! Yes, she can do that for me."

So, even while the "what do I do now" question loomed over me, I began to realize something. Okay, here's the scene. I'm out there. I meet someone. Then there's that messy business of engagement. I don't mean engagement as in proposing. I mean conversing with someone new, and learning about each other, and "What do you do?", and "What do you like?", et cetera.

Eventually I get a feeling for the person based on choices she's made, problems she has, and dreams she's shared. And so, one date works, and another doesn't. But then there's that special one. The one that just clicks. And I say to myself, "Ya. This one feels right. This one is easy and comfortable. This one " has what I need."

BOOM! "... has what I need." Those words rang like a cannon shot across the bow of my mind.

Suddenly, I feel like I am being warned. Okay then, time for a quick assessment. Here I am, very hesitantly entering into the single scene, and suddenly seeing a pattern. Yes, here was a new woman, but was she really? Wasn't she a lot like my exes? Was I just following a pattern I had established many years ago? Oh, maybe the kids were grown and gone, or the financial situation was different (those external things), but the emotional gravity that existed in my first two marriages was again rising from the ashes with this new woman. New woman, old pattern...and here I am falling headlong into it again. BOOM!

I had to stop and take stock. What I found was that I had cast in concrete certain mind patterns of how a relationship should be. And then I'd gotten myself into bondage to those thoughts.

I began to see this pattern in other areas of my life. Like in business associations. I was always helping new or failing businesses. I would help them to get going but would inevitably get sucked into each of their unique dramas. They would struggle, and I'd be right there, struggling along with them, sticking with them to a point that was way beyond helping. This compassion I had for others had turned into a noose that slowly choked the life out of me and my associates.

How could that be? After all, wasn't compassion a good thing?

WOW...still at "what do I do now". Here I was, a self-proclaimed follower of Jesus. Yet I had become dependent on other people's wants, and on trying to fulfill those wants by myself. Of course I would fail every time, and in the case of marriage it led to divorce.

In the new testament the apostle Paul makes a hard statement. He says to forget the things of the past and look to the mark that is in front of you (Phil 3:13). It's also my understanding that God has forgiven all my sins, past, present, and future (Heb 10:12). I had always approached these biblical declarations from the standpoint that I was to avoid looking at the actions and sins of my past and instead look forward to new adventures and commissions.

But wait a second. I was having a revelation. It was becoming clear to me that, in the context of those teachings, I had never included consideration of the "ingrained thought patterns" that had been my driving force for years. My way of doing things, my repeating behaviors -- they were imbedded in my character. They were me in "the flesh". Everything I had been taught, everything I had discovered in Christ -- I had looked at through this behavioral flaw that I was living in.

"I began to view my thinking in a new light". I was shown that I must look back, even back to when I was in the occult, at all of my thinking and actions. Only then did I discover that my thoughts had been completely contrary to the goodness of God. The Holy Spirit showed me that Paul's statement wasn't just about forgetting and re-starting. "It was about discarding and renewing". My way of thinking and acting had to not only be put in the past and forgotten. It had to change. I had to change the way I thought and lived.

With this new insight I finally understood why both my personal and business relationships were not working. I had been caught in a cycle of repeating lifestyle, and I had been its creator. But now I knew it was time to move on. It was time to abandon my well-worn notion that love and marriage were about need and filling the need. My compassion was a good thing, as long as it came from the Kingdom in my heart, and not the Medom of my mind.

Perhaps you, reader, can identify with my life. I believe each of us wants to feel needed and loved. I believe that is a truth about mankind. God made us for relationship, but too often we get side-tracked by our earthly relationships. He made us, first and foremost, to have an intimate relationship with Him. To be totally dependent on Him. In my head I had known this.

But I found myself repeatedly getting into earthly unions where I could and would enable my partner to persist in unhealthy behaviors. I enabled by helping them where I perceived a need.

Such behavior on my part proved to be devastating. Because sooner or later, I would let my partner down. And once down, the door was open for hurt feelings and mistrust. How Satan can flip the best of intentions around without us even recognizing it!

You know what? I STILL must remain vigilant. Very recently, frustration came upon me simply because what I thought was a working relationship never was. AGAIN, I began just trying to be helpful. But from her perspective, my "helping" couldn't be trusted. The bond we tried to forge shattered, largely because it was based on the instability of my pre-revelation thought pattern.

What have I learned? Forget the things of the past. What things? Well, certainly the way I used to think and act. My mind is being renewed into the likeness of Christ. I can stop thinking the way I used to and start thinking like God. Once I captured this mystery of "Christ in us, the hope of glory", I have been on a journey that is seeing my mind renewed. On this journey, Christ brings things to my attention that need correcting. He is not doing this to me for my condemnation. And He is not whipping me because I think wrong thoughts. No, He does it out of love. He does it so that I may draw closer to Him. Closer -- into the type of intimacy He so desires to have with me. It happens by transformation.

As I live in this transformation, I see people in a wholly different way. Yes, God has placed compassion in me so that I may help them. But I see my helping in a different light now. It's become a "running alongside of them" in a way that builds and edifies. It is not to satisfy my own need. I am not that enabler who only succeeded in bolstering inadequacy in others. I am not the character builder. God is. And He will build people up, including me, using His own methods. I am present in people's lives but to direct them toward Jesus with the gifts He has given me.

Transformation can be tough, and I've got the scars to prove it. I lived that "old way" for decades. It was a lifestyle where I reacted with quick, instinctual, flesh-driven thoughts. But as I learn to respond to the Spirit, I step into the thoughts of God. In the waiting to respond, I allow myself to see the situation from God's eyes. During this time of waiting I have a choice to make.

Do I want to muddle through in my perception? Or will I let the love in His eyes be my vision?

Changing the patterns, we have engaged in for years can bring us into relationships abounding with truth, joy, and peace. Knowing this, I have begun making long lasting decisions that will affect the rest of my life. I am now choosing to be with people that do not bring me down. I choose not to be in a relationship where I enable 'the one I love' to continue making harmful choices. I am not choosing relationships that require my strength to pull partners out of their own mire. I am not that person that has all the answers or even thinks I have them. In fact, I choose not to be the answer man. God has the answers. I can help only by pointing to Him.

What do I do now? I choose relationships where I am free to respond with the care and love I see in the eyes of my heavenly Father.

CHAPTER EIGHT:
THE MYSTERY OF BEING HUMAN

Have you ever wondered who began calling us "human beings"? Follow me, if you will, down a short rabbit trail of trivia for the answer.

It's the 14th century, and the Roman Catholic church is the predominant power in the world. The Church is also the world's primary educator regarding things Christian. As the religious hierarchy studied the scriptures, they noticed that God *and* the angels were both referred to as "beings". The thinking before this had been that only God was worthy of the title "being". But they deduced that since God had *created* the angels, and God's Word described angels as "beings", then God's other *creation,* namely Adam, must also warrant the title of "being". And hence, being a human (which means "man of the earth"), we became ***human beings***.

I've asked you to ponder this question so that I may illustrate a point. And it is this: that once we are reborn in Christ, we are partakers of all the attributes that compose the Godhead. Because our *being* is united with His *being*.

That means that if God is a creator, then so are we! We have the creative power of God in our being. Just as we have His life and His love. Just as we have His faith and His devotion. But back to the creating part…. I've realized that *my creative process is the living of my life.* It's embodied in my furtherment, my progression, my refinement. In Him, I help create the Kingdom! Conversely, to stop creating is to adopt a cemetery mentality. It's a retreat into Medom. If I stop moving forward, if I choose stagnation, then I live a defeated unGod-like life. *The life* is in the new creation I am in Christ, who lives through me, AS ME. It's a gift from God -- this "being" -- this human BEING and CREATING and LIVING.

Now let's take the word "rest". It's a word we see almost immediately in the bible, as God rested on the 7th day (Gen 2:2). It's obviously a term of considerable importance. Likewise, Jesus rested when He proclaimed "It is finished!" at his crucifixion. God rests. Jesus rests. And because I am one Spirit with Him, resting is who I am also.

Creation *and* rest. All at once and for all time. God, living outside of time -- living in the present, the past, and the future. Thus I am realizing that the creativeness of God and man never stops. God lives creatively. And I, as a human being, reborn of the spirit in Jesus, and also living ever-presently -- am forever creative. As I commune with God, I live in a creative mode. And it's in that creative presence that I rest. The creation is ever-ongoing and I rest in that. The creation and the rest are eternal and are always God's will. My resting and creating is my testimony! It involves no performance or work on my part. I don't have to keep up with everyone's drama. I don't have to react to my flesh. Rather, I have entered an eternal world, and only do what God has in His mind for me. I have the mind of Christ. I know God's will for me as He permeates my being. So by Him and through me we create His will here on this earth. It's God's Kingdom come on earth as it is in heaven! Through our connection with Him we create the Kingdom here on earth!

By now you may be asking, "What does any of this have to do with the divorcee?" The answer is "Everything!!!"

Life during a divorce can seem like an endless series of misguided deeds. I know it did for me. Selfishness grabbed center stage as my dreams and desires expired. I alternately struggled with blame and forgiveness. Lusts forced themselves upon my brain, and old thinking patterns compromised my behavior and my decisions. During the divorce I found myself dealing with all these types of worldly matters.

But in spite of getting caught in all that worldly whirl, one imperative never changed for me. And that was this: that if I am recreated in God's image, and if Christ lives in me, **then my eventual response will be to see myself as God sees me**.

Most people think that how they *see* themselves is how they *are*. Their identity is determined by their circumstances. For example, during my divorce and all its tribulation, I could have determined my identity by the way I was acting. I could have easily been resigned to just muddling along until the day I died. After all, hadn't I been acting selfishly? Hadn't I been riddled by guilt and covetousness? Hadn't I made one bad decision after another? It could have seemed that *the real me,* a me I wasn't too happy with, had finally bubbled to the surface.

Or...

I could have thought that those traits I found so distasteful or even detestable, were only a *part* of who I was. I mean,

I was also a Christian! Didn't I have Jesus there to help me when I could not help myself? Even though I was acting quite sadly, didn't I have God as my internal cleanser when I got dirty? It would have been just as easy to *see my behavior*, and at the same time *see my salvation*, and conclude that sometimes I'm bad and sometimes I'm good. I could have believed that the *real me* was a mixture of both.

Or...

Is it possible that I might be something other than either of those choices? Could there be a third choice? One that is not seen, but *known*. Might I be, as the scriptures say, "...seated with Christ in the heavenly realms..." (Eph 2:6)? **Can I accept that in this life there is both good stuff and bad stuff, yet realize the spiritual reality of who I am to God?** Yes! I can say yes! I can say that even though I don't look like it, and even though I don't feel like it, I choose to believe that I am who God says I am.

So now I'm asking you, reader -- what does He think of you? Now remember that He created you. He wants to give you all of His character which is good, lovely, and full of peace. That's what He sees in you. He loves you regardless of what you have or haven't done. If you did nothing more on this earth, He could not love you more, for His love for you is without measure and boundless. Even if you don't believe in Jesus, God still loves you. But when you believe in Jesus, God puts you on the throne with Christ.

Staying focused on how God sees us has an overwhelming effect on our lives. His love moves us from restlessness to rest. And His creativeness moves us into eternal reality. This is the transformation of our minds. The wonderful safety net in all this is that even when we take a few steps back or mess up, *God still loves us.* God has always had our best interest in His heart. His whole purpose when He created us was to have fellowship with Him. So, through all the differing situations of our lives, including the ugly ones, *even divorce*, God is beckoning to us. The trials we encounter constantly awaken us to the supernatural reality of Him in us. He wants an intimate relationship with us so we can become totally immersed in His love for us.

I now look at my divorce as part of my adventure with God. Because of my divorce I have a more intimate relationship with Him, and I am seeing others as He sees them. While married, I was living in Medom. Did God like it when I settled for divorce? No. God wants marriage to last. Did I make some bad choices? Yes. Yet He loves me and wants the best for me even if I blow it. God has always had my back, my front, and my middle, because it's His character to care for me regardless of anything I've said or done.

This had always been a mystery to me, since I live in a fallen world where bad stuff happens. Sometimes it's happening to me. Sometimes the mystery is that I seem to be the source of the bad stuff happening to me! But the mystery is solved by His never ending care for me. It's solved in His willingness to abide in me, so that I may live above and not in the middle of the mess caused by my decisions.

I have been recreated in God's image as I believe in Jesus. I have become the apple of His eye and He dances over me. I have been made righteous and I am His friend. I am a masterpiece, as is each one of us in Christ (Eph 2:10). The more I remember God's evaluation of me, the more my former opinions and behaviors fade into my past. The more I embrace God's vision of me, the more my spiritual reality is established on this earth in this life. My mind and body are being restored. The true meaning of "restoration" is "better than the original". Thus I am walking in a newness that has never been before, in a creative lifestyle that bears the resemblance of God.

The turmoil I used to create from viewing my divorce through *my* eyes has ceased. No longer do I criticize, condemn, judge, or blame myself because of looking at my life from *my* perspective. No more do I see my divorce as a reason to shrink or hide. It no longer shackles or shames me. I no longer feel sentenced by a guilty conscience. Instead, I am at peace with how God created me and for what reason. I am esteemed because of His greatness, and it's my honor to honor Him. His love is being shared through me in my sphere of influence. And I am content to believe what God thinks of me, and not what I used to think of myself.

God is not interested in whether I am divorced or not (Heb 8:12). He is more interested in my moving forward. As I connect with this new mindset I can look at my past with an attitude of love and understanding. Moment to moment, I see what I have done through the eyes of Jesus, not my own -- and I can move on with my life enveloped in the refreshing love of the Father.

I have abandoned my patterns of the past. I am no longer attracted to women in need. I am aware that I sought those women so that I could satisfy a need in me...to help them...because I had to help. Those relationships, based in neediness, always turned sour. Now I look and respond to coupling possibilities as directed by the Holy Spirit. Yes, I employ boundaries. I use boundaries so that I might catch myself when heading in the wrong direction. Those boundaries are girded by God's love and might. I no longer respond to her neediness, or mine, but to the prompting of He who is in me. Being without those boundaries caused me and someone else a lot of pain.

Knowing I have a new found freedom from old patterns, I am assured that my future is bright. I am in Him that protects me from harm. I am in Him that directs my path. But best of all, I am at peace with myself. I no longer live under the guilt of my past affairs, but live in the love of my heavenly Father. I AM a supernatural human being in Christ, and life is no longer a mystery to me.

CHAPTER NINE: GETTING TO KNOW ME

One thing I've always known about me is that I'm somewhat of a romantic. And I associate that romanticism with my thorough enjoyment of music. Now it just so happens that one of my favorite tunes has always been *Getting To Know You*, by Oscar Hammerstein II, from *The King And I*. For me it embodies the sheer joy that comes from really knowing someone in a relationship.

But while on this walk -- this divorce walk, that is -- I have come to realize that in order to really know someone else, I must first really know myself.

It's interesting to me that whenever we speak of marriage, we talk about how *two* become *one*. But there is an important caveat regarding this sacred union. And that is this: that when the two are united, they are not blended so that either identity is lost. Rather, it is a commingling whereby each identity is enhanced.

In hindsight, I now see how very much I took on the character of my mate. I took it on so much that her every need became my need. And meeting those needs consumed me. I became obsessed with always trying to anticipate and fulfill my wife's desires. I can tell you -- that was a full-time job! And because it was full-time, it left no time for me. Somewhere in all my attempts to complete her, **I lost me**.

This proclivity to adopt the needs of others as my own spilled over into my professional life. I became a chameleon. With each new client I would adapt my business to suit their needs and wants. I became an expert at deciphering a client's character, and then molding myself to be that character. It seemed at the time like a good way to build a business. I knew what I did for a living and knew it very well. It was no problem for me to capitulate to each individual's demands. Except that in doing so, the business ceased being **my** business. It no longer bore any resemblance to me. I had lost myself in the characters of my clients.

The longer these conditions persisted, the more my own needs were neglected. I had lost myself in both my marriage and my business. If I'd had the wherewithal to ask myself, "Do I know who I am?", I would have also had to emphatically answer, "NO!". In both my marital relationship and professional world *I knew who people wanted me to be. But I had no idea who I was.* I knew very well what to do and how to do it when it came to others, but that was the end of the road for me.

A couple of years ago I entered into a project with my adult daughter. In the midst of this project, she suddenly made a statement that spun my head around -- and around and around! And around again because I had a difficult time understanding what she meant by it. Her statement, delivered simply and succinctly, was that I was so tied up with my wife and fixing her needs that I had no awareness of anything else ***including her***. Wham! When it finally sank in, it was like a right cross to my jaw! I wasn't only neglecting myself. My character assimilation had progressed to the point of neglecting other loved ones in my life. I had nothing left to give my own daughter. It was a wake-up call I needed, and I honor my daughter for her willingness to be truthful with me. She knew that my wake-up was going to take some time, and that I was still a long way from 'smelling the roses'.

I have seen this same progression happen in many marriages. Where one partner or the other falls prey to the notion that they must become what the other wants them to be. Where one partner thinks that if they just try harder to meet the other's needs, then all will be well. **It's erroneous** to believe that if I devote all my time, energy, and resources to fulfilling my partner's needs that I myself will be fulfilled. **It's a lie** to reason that in completely knowing my partner, I will better know myself. That kind of reasoning is a trap; a trap that will ensnare me, bury me, and forget me. I will be a partner without an identity.

I mentioned earlier in these pages that I had to get away and spend some time alone in Vermont. It was while there that I started to internalize the immensity of what had happened to *me*. First, I had become utterly lost in someone else. And despite my best intentions, that path had ended in bitter disillusionment. I realized I did not know myself. Then, in going through the divorce, all those best intentions, hopes, and dreams were stripped away. That was a scary place to be. I felt naked and exposed. *Who was I?* Yes, I knew what I did. I knew my behavior, my actions, my vocation, even my motives. But I knew I had to get deeper than that. There was more to me than that.

My meditations took me back to some things I knew to be vital and true. I knew that God had created me. Too, I knew that He had a plan for my life, and that peace and hope were in my future. I knew that. *But what bugged me was I was not living it.* I knew that my loving Creator had this peace and hope for me, but I was not experiencing it. So I had to ask myself, "Why? If this is true, why is it not happening for me?"

The answer was spoken in such softness -- more a hush than a trumpet: "Because you do not know who you are in me. How can you walk in what I have for you when you do not know who you really are? You know the gifting I have for you. You know how to flow in those gifts. *But do you know who you are IN ME?"*

"...IN ME." It was a startling revelation. And at first my reaction was just "WHAT?!" But after awhile I started to see the path I was now on...a path that never ends...a path in the I AM. And so "I WHO AM" sunk into my heart to stay. My spirit realm -- my innermost man -- is who I really am. And that will never change. I am in Him who is eternal.

You see, for so long I had been a victim of wrong thinking. I had believed that it was my trials that made me who I was. I thought it was my circumstances that shaped me. I even thought my heartaches played their part in making me who I was. That way of thinking leads us into a life of instability. That way of living depends on us changing from situation to situation. So when we are doing great, we think life is great. But when we're not, we think life is lousy.

It's what I call the Ferris Wheel Life. First we pay to get on the Ferris Wheel. Maybe we pay with a marriage. Maybe we pay with a divorce. Either way, we get on the Wheel and we ride. Maybe we think the ride is wonderful, maybe not. But soon enough, the ride ends and we have to get off. And we have to pay to get on again. Maybe we pay with a song of praise. Maybe we pay with depression. Either way, we get on the Wheel and we ride. Maybe we're filled with elation. Maybe we're filled with dread. At some point we must once again get off the ride and find a new way to pay. Because we can't let the Wheel stop. We can't let it stop because we still believe it's our life. We find an effort to indulge in so that it never stops. The power to run the Ferris Wheel Life always comes from us. We do something. We pay. We ride up and down and in circles. Until we are exhausted and the ride ends. And we look for a new circumstance to fuel the Wheel. Depending on the circumstance, it could be a long ride or a short ride. But it will always be changing, the ride will end, and we'll have to produce yet another ticket to get it moving again. *Because the Ferris Wheel Life depends on US DOING SOMETHING, rather than on **resting in the I AM**.* As I rest in Him, the lure of the Ferris Wheel Life disappears.

My meditations also led me to ponder how God thinks of me. I saw that if God so willed to create me in His image, then He must really like me. I saw that if Jesus died for me, He must really love me. And it was revealed to me that just like the previous assertions are unabashedly true, it also follows that EVERYTHING God says about "me in Him" is true. I have been reborn as a spirit man in His image. That Spirit, given to me freely, resides in me, and I in It. I am learning to live in who I am in Him which is of the Spirit realm and not of the natural realm. I caught hold of the truth that God cares for me so much that His desire is to be united with me in Spirit, and no longer separated by my flesh. Christ's obedience has made that possible. And I realized what God's Grace really was. It all goes back to how God views me. It's not based on what I do.

It's not even about what I think of my life. It's about what He thinks of me.

Catching this truth, my heavenly Father began placing key people in my path. Those key people were *living* this truth, and experiencing life in the I AM. They were people that had grasped the scriptures and no longer lived in the past. They had forsaken their past to live fully in the presence of Him.

This truth is rocking my world. I started to think of myself the way God thinks of me. I started *living* the way God thinks of me. I am a new creation. I am the righteousness of God. I do not live in condemnation. These statements, based on WHO WE ARE IN JESUS CHRIST, reflect how God thinks of you and I in the present tense. God -- who exists outside of time; who is fully existent in the past, present, and future -- has and will always think of ME as these things. Whether I screw up or not, and no matter how many times I pay to get on the Ferris Wheel -- God's thoughts about me are *unchanging.*

Now, as I believe, receive, and confess these truths of who I am in Jesus, I'm experiencing a change in how I think. Remarkably, my thoughts about *other people* are changing. I have received the knowledge that the way God sees me is the way He sees everyone else! His supreme desire is to be in personal relationship with each one of us because He sees each one of us as being supremely grand!

I began living this, breathing this, day by day, seeing others as He see them. Jesus loves through me, as me, because He is love. And our flesh becomes transformed into His likeness.

No more Ferris Wheel drama. No more making people into what we want them to be. No more judging people. Instead, our vision becomes the same as God's vision.

It is so important for me to know the character that God has given to me. If I do not have that character set and established in my heart, then I will once again become subject to other people's thoughts and actions. I remember that life. It was no life at all. But I don't fault myself. I just did not know that my true identity was in Jesus. I did not know what God thought of me.

Now I know, and have a choice. Do I listen to the voices of people who would enslave me in their image? Or do I listen to God who frees me to be everything there is to be in the infinite I AM? It may seem like a simple question and answer. But in reality, we have all at one time or another tried to shape someone else for our own purpose. Or been forced into a mold that stifled us. Those choices had very real consequences. It is a choice to rely on God and believe in what He says we are. Those consequences are equally as real, but bathed in glory.

What joy to know a person myself, not in the way I used to know, but as how God in me knows!

CHAPTER TEN: INSIDE OUT

It is generally acknowledged in the world today and for centuries past, that Man is composed of three parts. Those parts are usually referred to as Spirit, Mind, and Body. The Spirit and the Body, that is our "Inner Being" and the "Physical Flesh" that encapsulates it, have few if any other names throughout history. Pretty much anyone who hears reference to the Spirit and the Body knows what is being talked about.

But the Mind. Now that's a little different. It seems that the Mind, or let's call it The Middle Part, has gone by a variety of names. The apostle Paul in the bible referred to the parts of man as "spirit and soul and body" (1 Thes 5:23). Various others have identified our psyche, our will, our emotions, or our thoughts, as "the part in the middle". My understanding is that The Middle Part is all of the above. The Soul is that part of a man composed of his mind, thoughts, will, and emotions.

But what's important about this for me is to remember the construction. Just how do those three parts fit together? So I stay aware that the Spirit is my core. My Soul and Body surround that core. **And I <u>live</u> from the inside out**.

I've written a lot in this book about transformation. And that's why I even bring up this subject. *Because when it comes to the topic of DIVORCE, it is my Soul that needs transforming.* In my Spirit, I'm good. I'm in union with God. Nothing can change that. For "...nothing in all of creation will ever be able to separate us from the love of God that is revealed in Christ Jesus our Lord." (Rom 8:39)

But the Soul...ah, the Soul. Do you remember the song, *Stuck in the Middle with You*, by Stealers Wheel? In one verse they sing, "Well I'm trying to make some sense of it all. But I can see it makes no sense at all." That's how I felt about my divorce. That's how I *felt*. There it is, that Soul part of me, expressing itself as an emotion, a *feeling*. Does it change the Spirit part of me? NO. Does it mean I'm unloved by God? NO. Does the divorce and all the ambiguous thoughts that came with it negate who I am in Christ? NO. NO. NO.

But does any of that mean I won't be tempted to walk down a road that looks rosy but only leads to dissatisfaction? The answer to that is also no. I will be tempted by the Flesh. And it's so easy to get on that emotional Ferris Wheel. I've been on it before. I KNOW that ride. I KNOW what it's like to let my Soul run wild with the thoughts aroused by my five senses. *It's what I did for decades!* For many years I lived from the perspective that my mind and body provided. And from that perspective I made some bad decisions. I screwed up. And I bore the results of those actions. Sometimes I'd get down on myself for the mistakes I'd made.

But the biggest mistake of all was that I always went back to the same perspective for a new answer. I always went back to Medom. I became entrenched in deadend habits and patterns sprouted from my Flesh and nurtured by my Soul. *It was the only answer to be found in Medom!* And so I persisted from the fallacy that I could find peace, joy, and love, from anything other than the Spirit. I know now from experience that I cannot change me. Only God can change me. And He does it from the Spirit that lives within me.

I was asked recently, "How do you tell the difference between what your heart says and what your mind says?" First, I want to remember that God gave me a new heart and Spirit when I first believed in His son, Jesus (refer to the prophetic word of Ezekiel 36:26). I have a new spirit from Day One when I believed. But the mind (or Soul)? Well, the mind is a *renewal* project. "...let there be a Spiritual renewal of your thoughts and attitudes," (Eph 4:23). In Medom, I had operated from a five sense realm that was constantly changing with emotions that were all over the place. So when I listened to my mind, there was never any consistency. Although I only had one brain, physically, I was nevertheless double-minded (or triple, or quadruple). The heart, which is really God's heart, is filled with unalterable tranquility. And that's how I tell the difference. It's the difference between shifting sands and bedrock; between confusion and order; between unsteady and steady.

So now I have a choice. I always have a choice. God gave me the choice. And it's this. Which voice do I listen to? I suggest listening to the voice of the Spirit. As I do so, I am directed into the actions which fulfill the desires of my heart. The answers we hear from God's heart will always be based in peace, not disturbance; love, not hate; and redemption, not condemnation.

I *live* from my *core*. And my core lives forever!

CHAPTER ELEVEN: THE LAST HURDLE

Have you ever watched the Summer Olympics? So many amazing athletes and events. So many amazing teams and individual sports. All requiring their own special training and preparation.

But for me there is one event that stands out. It stands out because it not only stands on its own, but because it also stands as a metaphor in ALL sporting events. In fact, it has also been used as a metaphor in life. It's even become a colloquialism of world culture.

That event is THE HURDLES.

Yes, the hurdles. The event that is a race unlike any other race. A uniquely different type of race that actually tries to *slow you down*. Ultimately, *the hurdles may even take you down, preventing you from finishing at all*.

Ah, the hurdles. You know what I mean. Other races are straightforward, with a starting line and a finish line. They are all about how *fast* you can get from point A to point B without impediment.

But not the hurdles. Sure, you're still supposed to go as fast as you can. But they put these obstacles in the way. They actually put blockades in the way. And there's no way around them. You're blocked on both sides by lane lines that if crossed can disqualify you. You can't go under. Only Mole Man can do that (I just made that superhero up). So it's either go over or go through. Over is the prefered method.

Have you ever seen anyone try to go *through* a hurdle? It's not a pretty sight. Oftentimes, even while trying the prefered 'going over' method, a hurdler will catch a knee, a shin, an ankle, or a foot. That hurts. Suddenly they are trying to maintain speed with a new scrape or cut on their leg. And even if no injury results, banging moving flesh into a stationary object is going to immediately slow one down. That's not the object of the race, now is it?

But the worst scenario by far is when a hurdler missteps and TRIPS over the hurdle. Tripping hurts the most. I've watched hurdlers FACE-PLANT into the track. The head snaps back. The nose gushes blood. The chin jars shut, the tongue is bitten, and teeth chip or dislodge. Elbows and wrists that were only meant to assist in gaining speed are suddenly jammed against the ground and sometimes bones are broken. In other words, THE HURDLER COMES TO A COMPLETE STOP.

Athletes get how hard the hurdles are. Athletes in every genre can relate to the hurdles. Because they've all had their own "hurdles" to surmount. Obstacles, big or small, that blocked them from their goal. Barriers, physical or mental, economical or cultural, that sometimes prevail over their efforts to achieve.

We ALL get that, right? I can't think of anyone that hasn't had at least one roadblock occur in their life. Because we've ALL encountered circumstances that try to TRIP US UP. We've all had to jump some hurdles, and sometimes, we've had to jump over a lot of them.

I can appreciate that. Getting divorced was just like that hurdles race. No sooner did I jump one hurdle then another one would appear. And another. AND ANOTHER. I've tried to describe many of those hurdles in this book. From being trapped behind Medom's moat, to wallowing in the past, to blaming and shaming myself, to wrestling with my flesh, to recovering from the carnal wreckage, to acknowledging my codependence, to discovering who I am -- and on and on and on. Until finally it appeared. Finally, I came upon it:

THE LAST HURDLE.

The last hurdle. Last sounds good. But make no mistake. It would prove to be a most formidable hurdle, maybe THE most formidable. In fact, it would have been easy to look at it and conclude it was impossible to get past. I mean, it was *SCARY*! And it most certainly had the potential to stop me dead in my tracks. It seemed that the most devastating hurdle had been saved for last. My divorce journey had very surely led me to a hurdle that could kill my desire to live.

My hurdle was *THE SERMON ON THE MOUNT*.

That's right. The sermon of sermons. The most famous one. The biggest sermon of all. Jesus, himself, preaching to the multitudes. With all that incredible content. All that incredible insight. The beatitudes. The salt and the light. Loving your enemies. Prayer, fasting, giving, knocking. And then all those teachings -- on the law, on anger, on vows, on possessions. And, lest I digress (or subconsciously avoid), let me not forget about the TEACHING ON DIVORCE.

Matthew verses 31 & 32 read, "You have heard that the law of Moses says, 'A man can divorce his wife by merely giving her a letter of divorce.' But I say that a man who divorces his wife, unless she has been unfaithful, causes her to commit adultery. And anyone who marries a divorced woman commits adultery."

Whoa! What? Wait -- adultery? C'mon Jesus, you're scaring me! What do you say about adultery? Are you saying that I'm responsible for making adulterers?

On adultery, in Matthew verses 27-29, Jesus says, "You have heard that the law of Moses says 'Do not commit adultery.' But I say, anyone who even looks at a woman with lust in his eye has already committed adultery with her in his heart. So if your eye--even if it is your good eye-- causes you to lust, gouge it out and throw it away. It is better for you to lose one part of your body than for your whole body **to be thrown into hell**," (my bold and italics).

Well. There you have it. I'm going to hell. *"...the bible tells me so...."* Because I am not about to undo my divorce OR gouge my eye out. I won't and I can't. I guess what's done is done. In the language of the hurdler, I've done a face-plant. I mean, these are the words of *Jesus*, the most forgiving man to ever walk on the planet. Even He has left no room for forgiveness here. It would seem there are some sins that can't be undone once they're committed. More from *The Sermon:* " A healthy tree produces good fruit, and an unhealthy tree produces bad fruit. A good tree can't produce bad fruit, and a bad tree can't produce good fruit. *So every tree that does not produce good fruit is chopped down and **thrown into the fire**,"* (again, my

72

bold and italics). It surely sounded like this tree, namely me, was headed for the pit.

I took the issue to my clergy. At the time, they really didn't have an answer for me. They tried to offer comfort, alluding that somehow, if I repented and did better in the future, I'd be rewarded. It all left me feeling so hollow. So DAMNED.

It seemed that no matter what I did, it wouldn't matter.

I didn't know how close I was to the truth.

But I couldn't know the whole truth until I fully understood that *Jesus wasn't talking TO ME*. *He was talking to the JEWS of that time. And the Jews of that time were still living under the COVENANT OF THE LAW. I don't!* *I live under the COVENANT OF GRACE, which was not established until Jesus died on the cross. The fact is I could never have been under the OLD COVENANT, because the Law was ONLY for the Jews. I, being a Gentile (that is, a non-Jew), have ONLY been offered the NEW COVENANT.*

Jesus wasn't talking to me! The Sermon on the Mount was from the mouth of a Jew to an assembly of Jews, all of whom were still under contract to uphold all 613 laws as dictated by God to His chosen people through Moses. Jesus was explaining the Law. He was preaching the Old Covenant.

Suddenly, another part of *The Sermon* made real sense to me. In Matthew 5:17, Jesus says, "Don't misunderstand why I have come. I did not come to abolish the law of

Moses or the writings of the prophets. No, I came to fulfill them." He came to fulfill the law. Why? Because we couldn't. There was simply no way we as humans could ever keep all the law. Heck, we couldn't even keep the BIG 10. So Jesus came to fulfill them for us. How and when did He do that? *When He died on the cross.*

It was at that moment, when Jesus died, that the Old Covenant ended and the New Covenant began. It was in that moment that WE **ALL** BECOME GOD'S CHOSEN PEOPLE; when "There is no longer Jew or Gentile, slave or free, male or female," but only those who being chosen, choose to be "one in Christ Jesus," (Gal 3:28). It was in that moment, that my salvation and deliverance was no longer based on my performance, but on the obedience of Christ. Jesus himself declared it, saying "It is finished," as He breathed His last. What was finished? The Age of Law. What began? The Age of Grace. The Father, in His infinite wisdom, had taken us out of the equation, knowing full well that we could never keep our end of the bargain under the Old Covenant. The Covenant of Law had been designed to show us that we needed help. We needed a savior. We needed Jesus. And it was by His sacrifice that our sins have been forgiven forever.

Hallelujah! I AM FORGIVEN!

Hallelujah! I AM NOT CONDEMNED!

Have I sinned? Yes. Have I transgressed? Yes. Does divorce fall into those categories? Yes. **Is it all covered by the blood of Jesus? YES!**

It's the last hurdle. And how about that -- I WOULD NOT HAVE GOTTEN OVER IT BY MYSELF. I had to receive Jesus. Now I can live each day in Romans 8:1, which states, "So now there is no condemnation for those who belong to Christ Jesus."

My forgiveness is not dependent on my behavior. Because no matter what I did, it wouldn't matter! What matters is what Christ did. All I need remember is that I live by His Grace. The Grace that fulfilled the law. The Grace that replaced the law. The Grace that guarantees my redemption.

CHAPTER TWELVE: FREEDOM ABOUNDS

"SURPRISE! You are going to be set FREE!"

Huh? What? Surprise?

Yes, surprise. Because I would never have imagined that this journey -- this journey out of divorce -- would end in freedom. I never dreamed that God's designed plan for me -- and for each one of us -- is to live a life of joy, peace, and completeness in spite of my sins. I was unaware that a life free from guilt, shame, and disapproval was always God's intended destination for me.

You see, all I knew was that I was divorced -- and for that, I was under a whole heap of self-condemnation. The only hope I had, the only thing I could see, was that *God would get me through* this horrendous experience.

But He spoke to me, gently. So gently I couldn't even hear it at first. I had all this NOISE in my head blocking my reception. But gently He continued. Gently He coaxed me to see this divorce through His eyes. And lo, *this journey has not just been about getting THROUGH it.* This journey has been one of amazing discovery, as I learn a whole new way of viewing and living life in the way that He desires.

I learned that above all, He created us to have fellowship with Him. His desire is to talk **with** us. And while He is forever patient, and will listen to us talk incessantly **at** Him about our perceived needs and frustrations, He desires more. He desires a created being that will also listen to Him. He desires that as we levy question after question upon Him, we will realize His perfect goodness and listen for His answer. Because He has the answers. He is not a God that holds back from us any good thing. It's His nature to respond lovingly to His children.

There is a rather common perception in Christian circles that after asking God a question, we have to wait for an answer. We're convinced that there are even times when we have to wait...and wait...and wait some more. Sometimes we even have to ask God the same question AGAIN, and start waiting all over AGAIN. I don't believe that. I DON'T BELIEVE THAT. In fact, I think it's absurd. Are we so arrogant that we think God doesn't know the answer immediately? Or that He needs to think on it before answering? Or maybe we have the (incorrect) belief that He's got a few different options, and depending on our worth He'll make a choice befitting us. THAT'S CRAZY. God's desire for each of us is to live life and have it abundantly! That never changes! So His response to us will never change either. He lives in us and He reveals mysteries to us. Therefore it is not logical that He would withhold answers to our questions. If we will but listen to Him that is in our hearts, we will discover that the answers we seek are already written there. So I believe that as soon as we ASK, our task is not to wait, but to LISTEN.

So is the problem with listening? Or is it with believing? Maybe it's both. I think so. **But as I believe more and more that my Father only wants what is best for me, I can then trust that the gentle voice I hear within me is Him**.

For example -- I was thinking about selling a business I owned. Eventually I sought His will, and felt led to ask

God, "Do I want to sell the business for my own personal reasons? Or am I being motivated out of concern for the woman I am about to marry?" Mind you -- I was listening. And the answer came back in a flash from within me...to sell it would be for selfish reasons. The answer burst upon me *in that moment*. I did not have to consider the question again.

Has that ever happened to you, reader? I think it happens far more that we acknowledge. So often we doubt that it is God speaking when we hear an answer to prayer. We tend to let fear reign in our brain instead of faith in our heart. Sometimes we may even think like this: "I didn't like that answer, God, so maybe if I pretend I didn't hear it, your answer will fade away." You see it really is a trust issue. Are we trusting in the One who dwells within us.

For my part, on this particular question, I *knew* that the answer given me had come from the inner Spirit that knows all about me. I didn't have to wait. I knew it was pointless to debate. The answer was there. My subsequent action on the aforementioned question was enveloped in total peace.

Our Father wants to answer, but so many times we do not listen. We misinterpret what it is *to commune*, or to be in communication, with God. It's not a one-way street -- it's two-way. Take Adam in the garden of Eden for example. God had spoken with Adam about not eating from the tree of the knowledge of good and evil. Adam listened and understood that as long as he left that tree alone, he would live in communion with his Father. But ultimately Adam decided *not* to listen to God's instructions, and instead to listen to the serpent. The immediate result was a fall from

Grace, and Adam seeking isolation. In his shame, the last thing he wanted to do was "fess up" and listen to God. At that point Adam was willing to forego any communication with his Father. He knew there were going to be consequences. But God's love is forever and unchanging. So He called to Adam after he had eaten the forbidden fruit. It wasn't until Adam *replied* to God's calls that communication began. It required receiving and responding. Had God spoken and then acted without first hearing from Adam, it could not be called communication. God obviously knew where Adam was, and even what he was thinking. But God's desire was that Adam would call back to begin a new dialogue with Him -- to begin listening once again.

There is no listening process until we receive and respond. There is no listening process if all I'm doing is just praying and acting. If when encountering a situation I don't listen for God's answer, then I am doomed to listen to myself. I am doomed to dwell in Medom, from which I will only get Medom answers. I believe that if I find I am pondering or analyzing a situation over and over, then what I'm really doing is isolating myself from God. I'm not listening! I'm not heeding the Holy Spirit within me! I'm acting like I'm on my own. And when I do that, I stop the flow of freedom that God desires for me through communion.

Jesus was asked by the crowds, "What must we do?" He responded, "Just believe," (my paraphrase, John 6:28-29). When we ask the same question today, are we not asked to respond with a like attitude of belief? Just believe that what comes out of us is from Him! It is no longer from the old self I was before Christ. Check the printed word of God and you will see that this reasoning is scriptually sound.

We are designed to live in belief that the Holy Spirit is constantly informing us of our Father's will for us. If we will adopt an attitude of listening and receiving His word, we will live more abundantly in a minute-to-minute reality that can only be characterized as a divine adventure.

As we walk out this adventure we will make plans. But we must always remember that the results are up to God. "We can make our plans, but the Lord determines our steps," (Prov 16:9). So as I plan I need to watch out! It can be very tempting to say, "I'm planning this…" only to follow it with "Okay, but *what if*…." *What if* can trap us in the future. We don't need to ask that question. God desires that we live in the present, not the future. As we live in the present, the future will take care of itself, "decently and in order," (1 Cor 14:40).

People love to do things the same way over and over again. They think if something is done differently then it's "out of order". They love to decry doing something in a new way as being "of confusion" and not of God. Hold on for a sec there! Throughout the bible are many examples of God doing some pretty crazy stuff! God was always amazing humankind with acts that defied description or explanation. But leave it to some religious zealot to get upset about it because it hadn't been done like that before!

How about we allow God to do whatever He wants to do. How about we don't judge. Because once we judge by what we think should take place, His desires are shut down in us. Then we are not freed. We're bound to the confines of Medom.

Today, because of this incredible journey I have walked through, I can honestly say that my former life does not affect the Spirit man within me anymore. All those former thoughts, deeds, transgressions, misgivings, trials, and denials...none affect who I am in the Spirit today. This is not to say that my actions don't sometimes bear resemblance to my old nature. But more and more, I am a reflection of the Spirit of God in me. I am alive in Christ. My thoughts are being transformed into the likeness of Christ that lives in me.

What a progression in my life from where I was when my divorce began. I am learning every day what an adventure this life is as I am being transformed into His likeness. I find I'm no longer living in the past, with its agonizing remorse and pitiful analyzation. Nor am I living in the future, wasting away in an effort to anticipate everyone's next move so that things might be how I want them to be. I am learning to LIVE IN TODAY JUST LIKE JESUS DOES.

Today I thank God for the new eyes that I see life through. Because of my new vision I am able to answer His call. I am listening. And I have become willing to change my way of thinking. I am being brought to an exciting place where freedom abounds. Freedom abounds in abiding in Christ! It's a place designed especially for me! One that brings out the best in me because of my union with Him. A place of security and peace; reliance and rest. A place where I draw in His breath, and breathe out His love.

I am convinced that He has that special place for each of us. Yes, the circumstances and the people may be different -- **but God's love is the same for us all.** So whether it be you or someone you know that is enduring the tremors of divorce, may we all be released to enjoy freedom in Him.

"And I pray that Christ will be more and more at home in your hearts as you trust in Him. May your roots go down deep into the soil of God's marvelous love. And may you have the power to understand, as all God's people should, how wide, how long, how high, and how deep His love really is." (Eph 3:17-18 NLT)

ABOUT THE AUTHORS

Peter was a sixties east coast hippie (Woodstock, ect.) and had a opinion of the church of being a social gathering place and nothing more. I was told by a Pastor that I asked too many questions and was not ready to join his church. I immediately dove in drugs, alcohol, and the occult. During this time I started my craft, as chef, and I climbed the professional ladder very quickly . After moving to southern California, as chef, I was abruptly stopped by Jesus showing up in my car one afternoon. I looked at Him and asked, " What the hell do you want from me?" He lovingly replied, " I want you". I went to the nearest church I knew of and read the scripture John 3 :17. Next day I was at a Vineyard church service and got healed of addictions, lower back stuff and stopped my profession all in one day. I have been living in Jesus since. Years later I was faced with a divorce from my wife and business partner and God showed the way of Grace to live in the love He has for us and to release it upon the earth.

Michael Smith was born and raised in upstate New York. He has been active in Gods Kingdom since his early 40's. But it wasn't until his move to Myrtle Beach South Caronia, with his lovely wife Lisa, that he came to know the fullness of grace. Members of Grace life Fellowship, a brotherhood of believers experiencing all the freedom and promises of Christ's finish work.

We would be honored
to share more with you individually,
or at your small gathering.

Please contact Peter at
petersinish1@gmail.com
or Michael at
mixmyth8@gmail.com
with any questions or comments.
We look forward to hearing from you.

If you are ever in Myrtle Beach, South
Carolina,
we are members of
GRACELIFE Fellowship & Ministries,
which meets for Sunday Service at The
Hampton Inn, 11:30am,located at 1803 S
Ocean Blvd, Myrtle Beach SC 29577
WWW.GRACELIFEMB.COM
Pastors Rick Sarver & David Hawkins
You can also watch current and past services
on
Facebook LIVE
at Rick Sarver's facebook account

Made in the USA
Middletown, DE
20 March 2023

27180576R00050